Thank you. Check also our other b

ASIN: B09ZCSW5SY

↑

Enter this ASIN in the search engine

A Very Easy and Exciting Exploration for the Youngest Kids about Diversity, Kindness, Respect, and Empathy

WE 'RE ALL ONE BIG FAMILY

BODY PARTS

© 2022 Misio Publishing

OUR TONGUES CAN DISTINGUISH BETWEEN FLAVORS

THE EAR ALLOWS YOU TO HEAR DIFFERENT SOUNDS

PEOPLE HAVE DIFFERENT EYE COLORS

YOUR NOSE HELPS YOU DISTINGUISH BETWEEN SMELLS

TEETH HELP YOU CHEW
AND DIGEST FOOD

WATER DOES NOT GET DIRECTLY INTO THE EYES WHEN IT RAINS. YOUR EYEBROWS STOP IT

SOME PEOPLE HAVE STRAIGHT HAIR. SOME PEOPLE HAVE CURLY HAIR. HAIR HAS DIFFERENT COLORS

THE NECK CONNECTS THE HEAD WITH THE BODY

DO YOU KNOW WHO HAS THE LONGEST NECK IN THE WORLD?

THE SHOULDER MUSCLES HELP YOU PERFORM A WIDE RANGE OF MOVEMENTS

THE CHIN IS CRITICAL TO CHEWING FOOD

YOU CAN BEND YOUR ARM,
ROTATE IT, SWING IT BACK AND
FORTH, AND MOVE FROM
SIDE TO SIDE

YOU HAVE FIVE FINGERS ON EACH HAND AND EACH FOOT. COUNT THEM ALL!

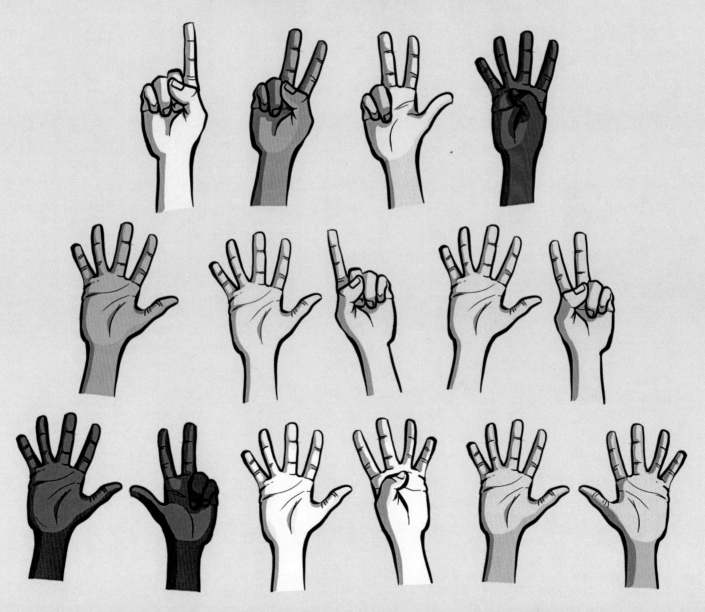

THE CHEST IS LOCATED BETWEEN THE NECK AND THE BELLY. TOUCH YOUR CHEST IN THE MIDDLE AND FEEL YOUR HEART BEATING

THE STOMACH IS WHERE THE FOOD GOES

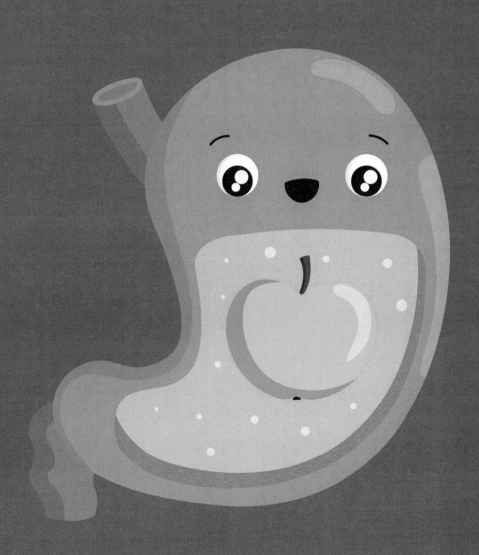

THE LEGS ALLOW YOU TO STAND, WALK, RUN AND JUMP

YOUR KNEE SUPPORTS YOUR BODY IN AN UPRIGHT POSITION. IT CONNECTS THE LOWER AND UPPER LEG

FIND YOUR HEEL! THE HEEL IS THE REAR PART OF THE HUMAN FOOT, BELOW THE ANKLE

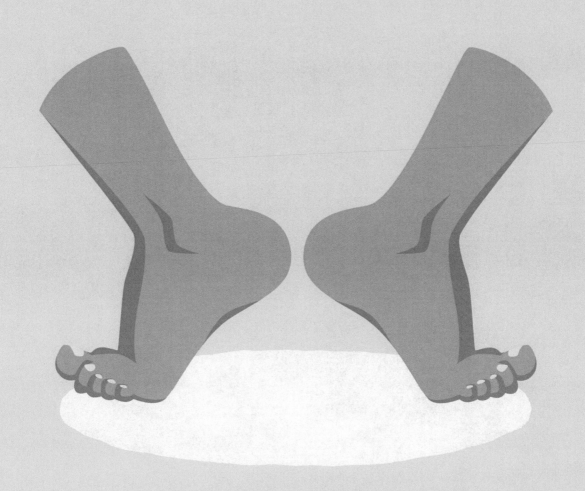

THE BOTTOM IS THE FLESHY PART OF YOUR BODY ON WHICH YOU SIT

TOES HELP YOU KEEP BALANCE WHEN YOU WALK

EACH PART OF THE BODY IS UNIQUE AND IMPORTANT. CAN YOU ALREADY RECOGNIZE THE ONES IN THE PICTURE?

WHERE IS THE EYEBROW?

WHERE ARE THE KNEES?

WHERE IS THE ARM?

WHERE IS THE NOSE?

WHERE ARE THE EYES?